Connecting with Crystals

Activate your natural intuition through divination with Crystals, Runes and Eclectic Collections.

Jenny Jo Allen

Copyright © 2015 Jenny Jo Allen

All rights reserved.

ISBN: 0692513094
ISBN-13: 978-0692513095

LOVINGLY DEDICATED TO

Jessica Macbeth

For setting such a powerful example with your many extraordinary talents: Healing, Teaching, Writing, Patience, and Faith. But most especially for encouraging me to share my own gifts through writing. Without that, this book would not exist.

CONTENTS

	Acknowledgments	i
	Preface	ii
1	What Makes Divination Stones Come to Life?	1
2	Clearing and Charging Stones	7
3	Layouts	25
4	Crystal Collections	35
5	Eclectic Collections	45
6	Rune Collections	49
7	Giving Readings	61
	Glossary	66
	Bibliography	67

ACKNOWLEDGMENTS

I wish to honor the spirits of the stones for gently nudging me, guiding my inspiration to deeply explore their connection to the infinite wisdom available to us all.

Thank you to my excellent editors, Philip Harrison and Colleen Maughan, and to Lucie Duclos for the beautiful cover design! I also love her artwork - check it out at www.duclosdesign.com.

I can hardly express the appreciation I feel for my husband Joseph Bayley, for honoring and encouraging my connection to Spirit. His endless support has allowed me to pursue many dreams. I am so grateful!

I would also like to thank my intuitive, curious and creative kids: Tara, Krispijn and Flora. Their beautiful spirits provide me with a constant source of inspiration and awe.

Last, but not least, I am grateful for my parents for their unconditional love, my clients for so many learning opportunities, and my generous friends whose positive responses to my earliest attempts at reading the stones kept me going.

♥ MANY BLESSINGS ♥

PREFACE

If you are seeking a clear path to working intuitively with crystals, you've come to the right place. This book will take you on a journey into the earth, connecting you with the energies of stones, minerals & metals through guided meditation. I invite you to explore the realm of expanded intuition through my step by step process of creating effective intentions. Discover new ways to express your creative connection to the intuitive realms by crafting your own personalized Rune symbols and meanings. Through my personal stories of success, failure and learning to listen to the whispers of stones, *Connecting with Crystals* is designed to help you embrace your true nature, illuminating your powerful connection to Spirit, as you open your heart and mind to the infinite wisdom all around you.

CONNECTING WITH CRYSTALS

1

WHAT MAKES DIVINATION STONES COME TO LIFE?

The use of stones as a psychic tool for divining and/or influencing the future is called Lithomancy. But, in layman's terms we call the act of casting and interpreting stones a "reading".

Reading crystals, stones and other small objects is similar to reading anything else (cards, tea leaves, bones, etc.). What is different, though, is the energetic quality unique to crystals and other stones that maintains an open portal to the Spirit Realm, all on their own. By deeply listening to crystals and aligning our energy with theirs, we can access that realm through the crystals' portal. Interestingly, when crystals are combined with other objects in a divination set, the other objects align with the combined energy of the oracle group, becoming nearly as active as the crystals. Therefore, throughout this book the word "stone" will include any small object that is used for divination in an oracle set of Crystals, Runes, or Eclectic Items.

What is "pure intention" and how is it used?

The trick to being successful in reading any oracle is to form a strong inner connection with that oracle. Creating your own stone divination tools with pure intention is a powerful way to form that connection.

Intention, as I will use it in this book, is the opposite of *will*. Will is used to *make* things happen, intention opens the flow of *allowing* things to happen.

Have you ever had to smile when you didn't really feel like it? A forced smile is an example of will – it takes effort. Technically you were smiling, but you probably didn't fool anyone into thinking you were happy because what makes a truly winning smile is the energy of it - the effortless glow of joy emanating from your smile and from you. That glow is the same effortless energy that is the flow of intention. When you relax and *allow* your energy to flow, you can *invite* that energy to move in a specific direction by using intention.

Although inviting intention is pretty easy, so is blocking it. Have you ever been in a situation where you wished a special someone would notice you? Imagine this; you are at a party and across the room you see your dream date. You long for this person to look up and notice you. You are doing all you can to send an energetic message of intention, but it just isn't working!

What went wrong? Well, a couple of things. If you really wanted your dream date to notice you, you should have walked up and started a conversation! But, energetically speaking, there are ways that we sometimes block intention. You will know if you are blocking intention by examining your feelings. This takes a little effort because you often have to dig under the surface feelings, or the feelings you *think* you are having to discover the hidden ones. Doubt, insecurity and frustration are some of the feelings that make you feel bad (insignificant, invisible, unworthy, etc.) and are effective intention blockers because they reside in the negative. The way to keep those blockers in check is to be in a state of openness, holding your intentions in a fully positive light.

For example, if your intention was, "I really want that hottie to turn around and fall in love with me at first sight!" it may seem like it is all positive, but there are needy attachments to that intention and you can bet they come from a place of insecurity and lack (obscured by the seemingly innocent surface feelings of desire). Alternatively, you could put it this way; "Universe, I am ready to experience a truly loving relationship with a fun, energetic, positive, intelligent partner who respects me and is worthy of my respect. I am open to receiving this person in the best possible way and in the most opportune timeframe. Thank you so much for providing a pathway to the fulfillment of this sincere desire!"

The first example is demanding and self-serving with neither respect nor gratitude. The second example is open hearted and full of possibility because there are no demands on how the intention is to be fulfilled. It is an open request for the best possible outcome. So… if the hottie really is "the one," and you have used pure intention, then they will also find you attractive. By using pure intention in this way, you will have linked yourself to the pathway of mutual attraction between yourself and your ideal partner. See how perfectly that works when you aren't trying to force it with *will*?

The Three Steps to Setting Successful Intentions

1) **Identify:** Clearly identify exactly what you are wanting, free of negative attachments and full of gratitude.

2) **Invite:** Open yourself to the love of the universe while you state your intention, being sure to infuse your intention with trust and gratitude for the best possible delivery and outcome.

3) **Receive:** Release all expectation of specific delivery (how it will be fulfilled) and prepare yourself to receive your intention in the best way possible by being open to what the universe provides.

I use this method every time I prepare for any sort of spiritual practice, to set up the parameters of what I am about to do. Before I begin a day of psychic readings and healing work, I set an intention for the space I am working in to be fully connected to heaven and earth, only inviting in that energy which is helpful, productive and fully aligned with the highest good. If I am away from my own building, I surround myself with the same intentions of safety and positive connection. I also set an intention for myself to be the most open channel for healing and helpful information possible and to be able to communicate that information in the most compassionate and effective way possible as well. I always express sincere, loving gratitude during and after my intentions – usually this is silent, but shout it out if that is more effective for you! Gratitude, aka love, is the currency of the Spirit Realm and usually the only necessary form of exchange for the help you are requesting, but feel free to ask.

The above examples are perfect for me. Now you create some that are perfect for you. Ask for what you want, give loving gratitude, then receive – it's easy!

When you create your own crystal divination set using this method of intention, you create a strong, personalized pathway to the unlimited information in the universe. As your relationship with your oracle unfolds and you develop a deeper understanding of the complex messages it provides, the intentional, creative energy you used to ignite your oracle expands inside of you…and your intuition expands with it. That expanding, intentional, creative relationship is what makes divination stones come to life.

"…and in the end, the love you take, is equal to the love you make…"

-The Beatles

Overcoming Low Self-Esteem is a Journey

One of the most common threads among my female clients is the issue of low self-esteem. It really isn't our fault. As women, we are a product of a patriarchal culture that teaches boys to be assertive and girls to be apologetic. I usually exude self-confidence, like to take risks and have pretty healthy boundaries, but even I have suffered from low self-esteem - without even realizing it! The following memories provide insight into my journey through the dark forest of low self-esteem and lack of support for my desire to fully embrace my intuitive nature. Perhaps they will assist your own journey to fulfillment.

Tarot cards seem to be the most accessible ready-made oracle. They are easy to find and come with a booklet that anyone can learn from. In college I played with several of my friends' decks and then bought my own. I tried for so many years to "figure my deck out" that I found myself in a bit of a slump, thinking, *Maybe I don't have the right deck, but probably I'm just not good at doing readings*. My Tarot deck was pretty, but I was never able to generate insight beyond the explanations that the author had written. My oracle and I didn't connect and sadly it collects dust to this day.

Even though I wasn't able to connect with that kind of oracle it didn't mean that I didn't have psychic ability. Some years later I discovered pendulums. I played with them for a while, which was great fun and they really responded to me (especially the ones with crystals in them) but I wanted to be able to do a more in-depth kind of reading and the more complex pendulum layouts seemed really difficult to learn, so my interest waned. My self-talk went like this: *The only oracle I am good at is the yes/no kind which must mean that I am not psychic enough to do "real" readings*. Isn't it amazing how we mess with ourselves?!

Fortunately, I learned how to access and trust my clairvoyant abilities through Reiki training and advanced Energy Work. And some years after that I recognized that I could connect to deeper spiritual guidance through crystals. My point here is not to allow your failed attempts (if you've had any) to cause you to feel insecure about your own abilities. Some people have a more difficult time tuning in to their psychic connection than others, and there are many different reasons for that, but I believe that we are *all* born with psychic ability – it is natural and normal, you just have to find the tools and techniques that work best for you and then gather the patience and diligence to develop your innate abilities. If you were drawn to this book, you are on your way to fully embracing your intuitive gifts – congratulations!

2

CLEARING AND CHARGING STONES

It is important to clear crystals and other stones of the energy they have collected while being harvested from the earth, processed, bought, sold and transported until finally ending up in your possession. They are travel-weary and in need of a spa treatment! Clearing out all that collected surface energy allows them to more powerfully resonate with their natural vibration. How often you clear your crystals depends on how they are used and whether their primary function is to emit energy, or to absorb it. As long as you only clear your crystals' surface energies and you give them some love afterwards, clearing your crystals as often as you sense that they need it will be just the right amount.

Charging crystals, however, is really only necessary if you intend to work with them in some way. Crystals are naturally active with the energy of their crystalline structure, so they will engage with their surroundings even if you do not charge them. Charging a crystal amplifies its natural qualities for the work you are agreeing to do together. When you charge a crystal, you align with it as a partner for a specific purpose. Crystals are power-houses of energy without being charged, but they are exponentially more potent when they are.

I have always loved stones, especially the colorful crystals that have a magical inner glow about them…mmmmm, yes, they do have that wonderful pull into the psychic dimension that I love…she says, gazing at a beautiful piece of milky blue Celestite and drifting blissfully away - then snapping back to reality… hmph!

Using pure intention while intuitively connecting with your stones is the most direct way to cleanse and charge them. After many years of study and practice it is pretty easy for me to slip into the intuitive realm, but if you are feeling like a few tips for how to access that realm would be helpful, this chapter will lead you through the process, step by step. Along the way you will learn how to identify your crystals' attributes, practice clearing and charging your stones, and develop a lasting bond as you learn the art of deep listening with your divination stones.

Step 1: Grounding and Earth-Sharing

Begin by "grounding" your energy. Sit in a chair with your feet flat on the floor and your spine as straight as possible, yet remain relaxed. With your eyes closed, breathe deeply and slowly through at least three breath cycles, relaxing your shoulders and allowing yourself to focus on the center of your body, just below your navel, as you breathe. Now imagine your feet sinking through the floor and into the Earth, down to your ankles. Breathe slowly in and out while you notice how your feet feel in the Earth. Now allow them to gently sink deeper into the Earth, past your ankles, while you are breathing…all the way to your knees. Feel the Earth's energy in your feet and legs while you are slowly breathing, in and out. Can you hear the Earth's deep gentle hum? Can you sense life in the Earth? See minerals? Taste water? Allow yourself to notice any Earth sensations you are experiencing.

Breathe in the Earth's energy, up through your feet and into your body. Exhale your busy mind energy down through your feet and into the Earth. Create a loop with your breath, sharing energy with the Earth. Slowly inhale the Earth's supportive energy up through your feet and exhale unwanted and excess energy down through your feet, again and again until you feel full, stable and relaxed. When you are ready, thank the Earth for sharing energy with you and open your eyes.

It may seem unfair to be sending your unwanted energy into the Earth, but it is just energy. We are the ones who put judgments like "unwanted, negative, or busy mind" on that energy. In the same way that trees happily absorb the carbon-dioxide that we exhale, the Earth will gladly take your "unwanted" energy as nourishment, especially if you offer it with loving kindness. When you intentionally share energy with the Earth in this way, you open yourself to the language of crystals, minerals and stones which are of the Earth. Deeply sharing with the Earth is the key to connecting with her treasures.

You can expand on the grounding and Earth energy sharing exercise by allowing yourself to sink in deeper each time you do it. We all have energy centers in the palms of our hands and in the soles of our feet. Practice opening the energy centers in the soles of your feet while your feet are deeply in the Earth and imagine roots, like tap roots from a tree reaching down through them, very deep into the earth. Then invite smaller roots to grow out from the sides of the tap roots in every direction, creating stability, strength and calm. Eventually, you can allow yourself to connect all the way to the core of the Earth, inviting the molten, golden liquid Earth energy to be drawn up your roots, filling your whole body with its warm glow.

Notice how your interactions with people and your life in general are effected when you start your day with grounding. If things are feeling crazy or upsetting during the day, give yourself a few moments to deeply ground your energy. The craziness may not stop, but your ability to handle it will be vastly improved!

Step 2: Expanding Higher Consciousness

Now that you are solidly connected to the earth you are ready to move on to expanding your awareness. Read through the following meditation and then take your own personalized journey into your higher consciousness. This meditation is my favorite and combines several journeys into one. Try breaking it up into a few different meditations to more deeply explore each journey and don't be afraid to adjust any part of it to suit your own needs.

This time, if it is comfortable for you to do so, stand with your feet shoulder width apart and notice that your legs are still deeply rooted in the Earth. (If you don't feel rooted, do the grounding exercise again.) With your focus on your center, breathe in and out, lovingly sharing energy with the Earth. Allow yourself to reach out through the energy centers in the soles of your feet with your tap roots and side roots until you sense a connection with Earth's crystals, minerals and stones. Invite that connection to become stronger. As you inhale, allow your breath to bring that connection up and into your heart-mind, filling you with love and the gift of perfect understanding. As you exhale, breathe that loving understanding back down into the Earth allowing it to connect with all of Earth's crystals, minerals and stones. Continue inhaling and exhaling, sharing yourself and receiving the stones, until you feel the gift of understanding filling up inside you and connecting you with all of Earth's crystals, minerals and stones.

Allow the Earth energy to stay in your lower body as you shift your attention to your Central Energy Channel; the open channel that runs along the inside of your spine connecting the energies of your body and spirit to the energies of the Earth below you and the Universe above you. Allow your attention to rise up your Central Energy Channel to your heart and breathe. Continue reaching up through your Central Energy Channel with your energy feet still planted firmly in the Earth and as you imagine your spirit body stretching up through the ceiling, reach up with your spirit, past the clouds and through the atmosphere and into our starry Milky Way galaxy. Pause here while you feel the vastness of the Universe. Feel your connection to all beings, all energies, all the information that ever was and ever will be. With your "energy eyes" look down your stretched body and feel yourself connected deep inside the Earth while you are still up in the Universe and know that the Earth is part of the Universe, as are you. Feel your interconnectedness with all of Earth's crystals, minerals and stones. Feel their connection with the Universe, through their connection with the Earth. Invite them to share their divine connection to the unlimited information in the Universe with you. Allow your intuition to feel that connection and to align with your place in the Earth/Spirit/Universe communication loop.

Take the time to notice any sensations or thoughts you are having that *don't* have to do with your busy every-day life. Allow those intuitive thoughts, words, sensations and/or sounds to take form. Follow their lead to see where they take you. You could follow a thought process, or allow a vision to unfold and progress, or you might hear sounds or have a strong sense of knowing about something. Perhaps you are visited by a spirit being who is taking you on a journey or showing you something of importance or giving you a gift. Allow yourself to receive any sensations or perceptions you are having, no matter how small or insignificant they may seem. Breathe into them and allow them to expand.

If you become afraid, ask what exactly is scary and allow yourself to receive the answer. Work through it if you can, or simply imagine putting up your hand in "stop" position. Go back to a happier place/thought/vision/sound and breathe.

When you are ready, thank all the energies in the Universe for helping you establish a strong connection to the unlimited information in the Universe through Earth's crystals, minerals and stones. Allow your focus to slowly come back down into the atmosphere, below the clouds, and all the way back down to your center. Thank yourself for allowing your spirit to travel such great distances and thank the Earth for assisting you in connecting with the unlimited information in the Universe through her crystals, minerals and stones. When you are ready, open your eyes feeling fully present and alive!

After a spiritual journey, take a few minutes to write down your experiences. Try to write down every detail. Later you will be amazed when you read it! Like dreams, these journeys tend to quickly fade away as you become fully present in your body and mind.

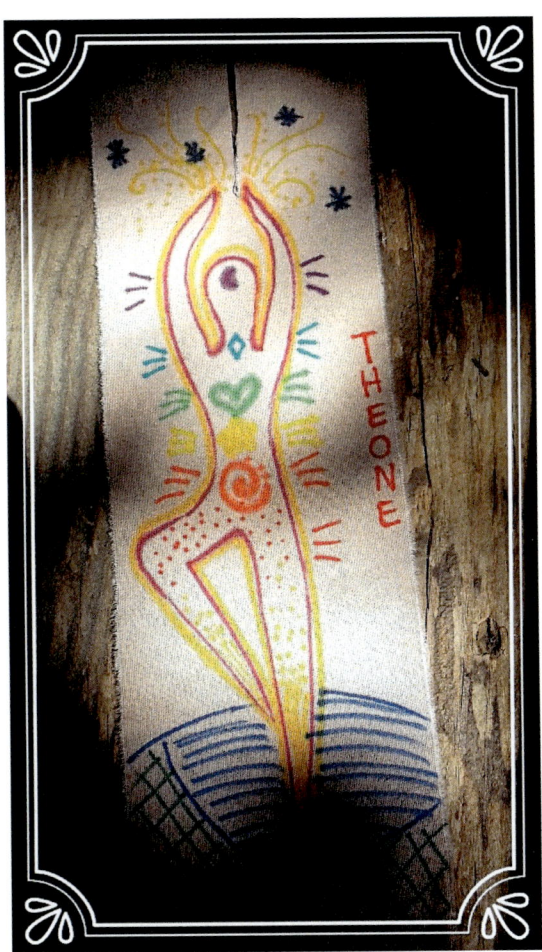

Step 3: Develop Your Intuition

When you clear or charge a stone, you will use intention. Intention is also closely linked to feelings and by extension, intuition.

From the first moment an intention enters your mind, your feelings are activated and energy moves. Remember, intention is not force or will, but allowing. This is a very important distinction to get because if you try to "will" your stones to clear or charge, it won't work. One difference between intention and will is that will takes effort and intention is effortless.

Take the Earth-sharing exercise we did for example; you used intention to "allow" your feet to fall through the floor and into the Earth. On the other hand, you might have had to use "will" to slow your breathing.

Intention is one way to access intuition. The flow of intuition is effortless and that first spark of inspired intention opens a pathway to intuition.

The meditation, *Expanding Higher Consciousness* (page 11), is a way for you to get acquainted with your intuitive abilities. How did you perceive information? Did you hear sounds or words? See visions? Feel sensations in your physical body or get feelings like joy or sadness? Did you just know things? At first, when you are seeing images or hearing guidance or feel that you know things, you might think you are "making this stuff up," but after a while you will be able to recognize the difference between what your mind is telling you and what your intuition - your connection to the unlimited information in the Universe - is allowing you to know.

One way to understand the difference is to notice how you feel when you get information. Feelings can be an amazingly accurate self-check system, but you have to be willing to be *really* honest with yourself. Is the information something you would have thought up, or did you feel a little surprised by the information? The feeling of interested surprise is a good indication that the information came from outside of your own thoughts. Did you come to a conclusion by way of a series of logical thoughts, or have a knee-jerk reaction caused by your own judgments and beliefs? This is probably not intuition! If you feel a sense of justification (here's the tough-love self-honesty part) it's a pretty safe bet that the information didn't come from intuition. Or did the information just pop into your head, seemingly of its own accord? This is often a sign of clear intuition.

I used to have a little battle with myself over whether or not I should tell my client what just came into my head, because either the messages didn't hold any meaning for me, or they seemed insignificant, presumptuous, or really "out there." Over time I have been able to identify which information is from me, and which is from intuition. Try to separate yourself from the judgments: "insignificant, presumptuous, out there," etc. Judgments are intuition blockers just like they are intention blockers. Notice when you are having judgments and say to them, "Thanks for sharing! Moving on!"

I think the hardest part of recognizing intuitive information is noticing when the information comes and not immediately casting it aside. Most of us have had the intuition culturally "beaten" out of us since childhood, but I guarantee, the more you practice using pure intention to access your intuition, the more clearly the messages will come, and the easier they will be to believe.

Step 4: Identifying Your Stone's Attributes

Before clearing and charging your crystal collection, you need to know what each stone will represent in your oracle readings.

There are a few ways to do this, but the method I encourage is to use intention and intuition to divine the meanings of the stones by "listening" to what *they* tell you they represent.

Other options are to use a crystal book, or research your collection's attributes online. If you choose to learn from others, it is best to reduce the long descriptions to a one or two word meaning for clarity. It is ideal to do this with your heart (allowing yourself to listen to intuition) rather than with your head (thinking hard about the descriptions and trying to figure out how to reduce them to one or two words). Reducing a description can be really challenging when there is a mile-long list of very different qualities attributed to each stone! Also, you are at the mercy of what someone else believes your stones should represent, just because they are called Jasper, or Aventurine, or whatever. From what I have observed, certain crystalline structures have a predisposition to energetically align with certain attributes (like love/relationships for Rose Quartz), but not always in the same way. My Rose Quartz told me it represented love and/or *primary relationship*, not relationships in general. That may seem insignificant right now, but while you are giving a reading it can make all the difference in the world! Also, if you begin to engage deeply with your stones now, honoring them by allowing their meanings to be "heard", you will be well on your way to successfully being able to read them as an oracle.

Step 5: Practice Deep Listening

I call this *deep listening*, but really I just mean *open yourself to receiving intuitive information*, because everyone receives information in different ways.

Any time you begin intuitive work it will go much easier for you if you are deeply grounded and then open your work with pure intention. (Refer to steps 1 & 2) After you are grounded, gather the stones you will be working with and create an intention (to God/Goddess, the Universe, or the stones themselves) that goes something like this:

"Please allow me to be the most open and receptive conduit for receiving the individual meanings for my divination stones during this deep listening session, and please provide the meanings in the easiest way for me to understand them. Thank you."

If a general intention isn't working for you, you could create an individualized intention each time you pick up a stone to divine its meaning. Try imagining that it is an adorable little kitten or puppy and talk to it with that kind of adoration and love. Go ahead and be sappy if it makes you feel good - feeling good is contagious, even to stones!

"Beautiful purple Amethyst, I appreciate you so much and I want to understand you to the best of my ability. Please share your primary meaning with me now. Thank you."

You don't have to say your intention out loud, but you do have to *feel* it – really mean it – in order for the stone to feel it. If the main attribute comes through before you say thank you, don't worry, just say it as soon as you are finished receiving. The really important part is to mean it when you are giving thanks.

With pen and paper nearby to record your findings, pick up your first crystal. While you are holding it and tuning in to its energy, notice your crystal's uniqueness, such as lines, clouds or clarity and color variations. Allow those features to "remind" you of something, then explore the meaning of that memory or idea to find the crystal's meaning.

When choosing a few crystals for my Eclectic Collection, I was really drawn to a specific piece of Celestite and when I began to look at it the part that really stood out for me was the line that sliced right through the center of it. *Cosmic Shift/Change* came clearly into my mind and it was one of my favorite crystals to work with until it split in two. Unfortunately, Celestite is a delicate crystal and the line inside it was the Cosmic Shift that earned it an early retirement! When I decided to attempt to replace it with another Celestite crystal, I wasn't sure if the next one would have the same meaning, so I made a request of the new Celestite to take the other one's place and it agreed! The new stone didn't have a line in it, and although it is showing some wear, I am thankful that I haven't had to replace it.

Another way to deeply listen is to hold the stone between your closed palms and *feel, know, hear*, or *see* its meaning. Being clairvoyant I *see*, so when I do this kind of deep listening with stones I notice when something flashes in my intuitive peripheral vision and then I focus in on the vision and the meaning of the visual images comes into my head as *knowing*. If you are having trouble with "hearing" some of your stones, they may be clouded by surface energies and need to be cleared first so you can more easily tune in to their natural vibration.

Learn more about your stone's qualities by noticing the light upon or within it; whether it radiates or seems to draw in energy. This will tell you if its primary function is to absorb or project energy. I have yet to meet a Rose Quartz that doesn't do both, though some seem to have a stronger affinity for one or the other. Rose Quartz is a healing crystal for emotions. It absorbs grief and projects love. But don't take my word for it…*listen!*

Tuning In

This journal entry from a student beautifully illustrates the "tuning in" experience:

"Today I collected stones on Clarke's Island and thought of how much they symbolically and energetically remind me of the billions of people on this earth… I experience a sense of knowing upon viewing and holding them… not in words, but in wisdom. Their energies come to me almost animatedly – but not quite – as though the most similar way my mind has to express what I sense is through comparing them to humans. I can get a sense of young or old, masculine or feminine, fiery or dull, thick or hazy, full or sparse, electric or dim, cheery or morose, naïve or wise, airy or earthen… or even warm, tropical, or fresh. Two stones that appear relatively similar and could be described through the visual sense nearly identically can resonate so differently. Stones are like humans. Each one so unique, and yet patterns are recognizable - all made of one set of minerals manifesting and combining in infinite ways."

– Miranda Hewlett

Miranda's example of opening up to the wisdom all around, no matter where we are, is so profound. Bringing spiritual awareness into everyday life and recognizing the interconnectedness of all, allows us to more easily access our intuition, because intuition is accessed through energetic connections. Start looking for signs of connection in the natural world as you move through your day. Reach out with your feelings and open yourself to receiving the whispered messages that are available to you.

"The greatest illusion of this world is the illusion of separation. Things you think are separate and different are actually one and the same."

~Guru Pathik, *Avatar the Last Airbender*

Step 6: Practice Clearing a Crystal

Once you have the meaning of your crystal figured out, hold the crystal in the center of the palm of your non-dominant hand and hold your dominant hand above it a few inches. Feel the energy connecting between your palms and through the stone and let the connection grow. Allow any distracting thoughts that come up to float away like clouds (*I wonder if I'm doing this right?*, or *OMG! I did it!*, or whatever).

When you feel ready, say out loud, "I ask that all of the surface energies that this stone has collected on its journey from the earth to my hands now be released so that its uninhibited primary meaning can have full freedom of expression. Thank you!"

As you say this, gently lift your top hand up and away, visualizing or feeling those surface energies lifting away from the stone and floating up to the heavens to be transformed for the highest and best good in the universe. Now your crystal is ready to be charged.

Step 7: Practice Charging a Crystal

Charging crystals by channeling energy into them is a beautiful way to increase their power for the work you are asking them to do. By sharing this loving energy connection with your crystals, you empower them, and yourself, for a specific purpose.

Refer to your notes from when you learned the meanings of your crystals, rather than going on memory, so that you charge them with the highest clarity. Hold the crystal in the center of your palm exactly like you did for clearing it. I like to charge each one right after I have cleared it because crystals *like* to hold energy and you are already connected to the crystal in your hand, so charging it will be easier and more powerful. Allow the crystal's meaning to flow through your heart, down your arms and into the stone. Say out loud,

"I ask that this crystal (say its name, e.g.; chevron amethyst) be fully empowered to channel (resolution of unhealthy patterns)." After charging them I like to give each crystal a kiss (sealed with a kiss!) to show my appreciation for its service to me. This also acts as a completion to the process and allows me to let go of the connection with that crystal so that I can move on to the next one. Another way to accomplish this is to thank the Earth for forming this beautiful crystal and thank the Spirits for all the guidance provided to bring you to this moment (or choose your own action/words).

"Thank you Mother Earth for creating this beautiful crystal and thank you to the flow of Spirit for all the guidance I have received to bring me to this moment."

There are many possibilities, but make sure that you find a sincere way to honor and release your connection to each crystal and to the Spirits (God/Goddess, Universe).

Step 8: Clearing Maintenance

Technically, as long as your crystals are performing to your satisfaction in readings, clearing is not required. However, crystals love to interact with other energetic beings and most will absorb energy. During readings your client will send their thoughts and feelings into the crystals. These are surface energies that do not affect a crystal's core meaning, but periodically the surface energies need to be released. If you never clear your crystals, they will eventually become difficult to read because they will be bogged down with all the surface energies of past clients.

On the other hand, crystals love to be loved and appreciated! Clearing rituals done with love and gratitude deepen the bond between you and your crystals, expanding your access to intuition through them. So, honor your stones often by clearing them and offering loving gratitude!

There are several ways to clear surface energies. The first three listed are commonly accepted and acceptable, but if you really want to open your pathways to intuition with crystals, I encourage you to give the last method (#4) some sincere effort, because really, the only effort needed is trusting your own intuition.

1) Bathe your stones in moonlight overnight. A full moon is the most powerful, but any moonlight is better than no moonlight.

2) Cleanse stones in salt water, preferably the ocean, but lovingly mixing sea salt in a glass bowl of purified water, rain water, or well water (and gently swishing the stones in it with pure intention) should neutralize surface energies.

3) Cleanse them in running water, like a stream or any natural outdoor flowing water, or allow rain to wash them outside.

One time I was at a friend's house and when we walked into the kitchen I noticed that her partner (also a good friend of mine) had set a medium sized black tourmaline crystal in the sink with running water from the tap splashing over it while he did other stuff. When I asked him about it, he said the person he got the crystal from said to cleanse it in running water. Sigh… This will, of course, not hurt a crystal and he was doing the best thing he knew how, but I felt sad for all the good drinking water down the drain and the crystal wasn't getting what it really needed to clear away the surface energies.

Moonlight, for example, is cosmically charged with a gentle reflection of the sun's too-intense cleansing energy. Ocean waves, even little ones, clear energy with movement and high alkalinity. Rain falling from the sky is highly charged with cleansing negative ions. Running water, from a babbling brook to a raging waterfall is full of lively, naturally energized cleansing. But, water from the tap…not so much!

4) The most powerful and accessible way to cleanse surface energies, is to get yourself deeply grounded and use your own amazing power of intention!

Holding the crystals in your hands, (all at once is fine after the initial surface energy cleansing that you did when you dedicated them to your oracle) ask for the surface energies that your crystals have collected to be released for the highest and best good in the universe. Lovingly imagine the energy lifting off your crystals and floating away, leaving them clean and fresh and vibrant. Thank the Spirits for their infinite wisdom and support and thank the stones for their continued service.

"I ask for the surface energies that these crystals have collected to now be released for the highest and best good in the universe and I offer my deep appreciation for this service. I also offer my deepest gratitude to these crystals for helping so many people find what they are looking for. Thank you."

As always, you are welcome to use my example intention, or create one that is meaningful for you. I know that I have created a powerful intention when I feel a sort of whoosh of energy flowing through me. In order to create that kind of power, it is imperative that your intention be full of meaning - and you are the only one who knows what is truly meaningful for you.

Clearing crystals and other stones of the energy they have collected is important because it allows them to more powerfully resonate with their natural vibration. It is also important for you to ritually connect with your crystals, keeping your mutual channels of intuitive information open and clear. Any stones that are part of your life, including jewelry, can be cleared and charged to increase your connection with them, and their ability to serve a common goal. Your stones are happy to work with you! If you deeply listen for the core gifts in each of your divination stones and enhance them by charging them with loving gratitude, you will forge an intuitive connection with your oracle that will shine the light of truth into every reading.

3

LAYOUTS
Drawing and Casting Techniques

A layout is the way in which the oracle is laid out during a reading. Though there are hundreds of possibilities for divination layouts, the ideas in this chapter are simple enough to learn quickly and flexible enough to grow in complexity as you become more fluent in your divination interpretations. With each style of layout there are suggestions to get you started. Further explorations of each kind of divination collection with specifics on how to do those readings are found in their respective chapters. I encourage you to use the suggestions in this chapter as a general guide, adjusting them to fit the divination set you are using and your own inner wisdom.

Two of the most popular divination stones today are Runes and Crystals. Traditional Runes were cast on a white cloth, which was quite practical a thousand plus years ago, and still has value today. Using a white cloth for casting was perfect for low-light conditions, offered contrast to dark colored stones, kept the stones clean and protected while casting and transporting, and was helpful in determining the boundaries of the reading.

I started out using an 11" circle of thin ribbon on an indigo blue cloth, but now prefer a 13" diameter circular cloth of my own design with dark velvet on one side and a Triple Subject Layout of intertwining different colored circles on the other.

If my client wants a general reading without any specifics to focus on, I choose the velvet side. The Triple Subject Layout offers a more complex reading to shed light on three areas of concern and how they overlap.

The following layout ideas are fairly interchangeable between Crystal Collections and Runes, and could probably be adapted for any collection of small divination objects.

Daily Draw

Doing a "daily draw" of a single Rune or Crystal in the morning provides meaning and focus as you move through your day.

Gently reach into the bag allowing your fingers to find the "right" stone and draw it out. Think about how its meaning applies to your life right now. If nothing comes to mind, think about how it could apply to your day. Create an intention, asking for the best possible experience or outcome of that meaning to apply to your day.

Quick Draw

Need a quick answer to a burning question? Do a past/present/future (PPF) reading by pulling three Runes or Crystals out of a bag after gently swishing them around while thinking of your question. The first one represents the past or origins of the question, the second stone represents the present situation and may include how to proceed, and the third represents the most likely outcome if you remain on your current path. If you don't like the probable outcome, change your path!

This is a PPF draw that I did with my Fairy Runes. It shows that in the Past there was great *prosperity*, the Present is a time of *reflecting* on that prosperity, and on one's current state of being, in order to attain the potential Future of *freedom*.

Casting Runes

When casting Runes you or your client can select a specific number of stones at random for the reading. Nine is a magical number in Norse mythology and thirteen is magical for Wiccans, but you can choose any number that seems appropriate. When they have all been selected, you can invite your client to cast (scatter or drop) them onto a cloth. If they land right side up the meaning is that of the symbol, upside down is a reversal of that symbol's meaning and face down can be read as being the probable outcome in the future. The reading will go much easier if there is a specific question or area of concern to focus on. From that focal point you can allow your intuition to provide additional information, giving depth and meaning to the reading.

Another way to do a Rune casting is to use all of the Runes in your collection. Have your client cast up to 13 stones at a time and if they are split into two casts, just have them drop the second batch on top of the first. The Runes that land symbol up are read and the others are ignored.

Or, try this one, invented by a student at one of my teen workshops – I tried it and it worked beautifully! After all the Runes are cast, take away and set aside the ones that landed symbol side up. Have your client pick up the Runes that landed symbol side down and cast them again. Now interpret the ones that land symbol side up.

No matter how you read your divination stones, make sure you decide how you are going to do it before they are cast. Prepare yourself and your stones by tuning in to the Divine with clarity and a pure intention for the highest and best outcome.

Casting Crystals

Casting Crystal Collections is done a little differently, but I invite you to explore all of the ideas in this book with any divination set. I have 20 stones in my Eclectic Collection and for a thorough reading I like to have the client cast them all. But 20 is really too many to hold at once, so I invite them to choose 10 crystals and while holding them in their hand I ask the client to allow their question to fill the crystals. I instruct them to cast the crystals by letting them fall from 6" - 8" above the center of the mat when they feel ready. Then I invite them to cast the remaining stones, right on top of the first batch, in the same way.

You can learn a lot about a person by how they cast the crystals. Some just go ahead and spread them all over, some carefully pile them up on top of each other no matter how I try to coach them with words like "scatter," but it's amazing how it doesn't really matter – they invariably cast them perfectly for their own most meaningful reading. I even had one guy telling me a story about himself and while he talked he chose various stones out of my bowl, thoughtfully placing them on the cloth in a sort of geometric pattern. The reading I gave him from those stones blew him away! What this tells me is that the client knows exactly what they need to hear, all you have to do is get out of their way during their casting process and then uncover the intuitive messages as represented by the stones.

The way I read divination crystals is governed by where they fall and what groupings they form. I look for "stories" in the groupings.

When casting a general reading on a single color cloth, there are many ways to set up the layout depending on what the client needs and what the situation is. In a public setting, like a psychic fair, I use a solid colored 13" circular mat and either give a shorter reading on a single subject chosen by the client, or give a longer general reading.

My general readings are pretty free-form, which requires a lot of intuitive interpretation, but these are some ideas for more structured reading layouts:

1) Have your client choose one stone as the centerpiece of the reading, this makes for an easy starting point for your intuitive interpretations and can be a guiding light for the whole reading, with everything else relating to the centerpiece. Have your client place that crystal in the center of the circle and cast the rest on top of it. You'll need to remember which one it was because often it is knocked into a new position when the rest of the stones are cast. If you have more than 13 stones, have them choose half and cast them, then let them cast the rest of the stones. You can just use the first set they choose for the entire reading, but I must admit, that has never worked well for me – my crystals are balanced and charged with the common goal of uncovering the knowledge that people hide from themselves, and it always feels like the story is incomplete if some are not cast.

2) You can use the circle as a clock with each "hour" creating a "slice of the clock's pie" and representing one week. Before the stones are cast decide silently where 12 o'clock is. I don't usually tell the client how I am determining the time-frame, because it is always best to check in with your intuition during the reading to make sure that the timing is accurate.

3) When reading the stones, the ones closest to the center seem to be the most active or prominent and the further out they land the more underlying or subtle they are.

4) Try this way to determine timing: the crystals closest to the center are telling the story of what is happening now or in the very near future. The further out the stones land the further in the future they will come to pass.

5) Allow the groupings of stones to indicate separate subjects and see if there is continuity between them and a natural sequence of events that will unfold. Sometimes I see a progression in the form of

a spiral, or there will be a fairly straight line that is separate from other groupings and looks like a progression. Don't be afraid to ask the client questions.

6) Consider alternate timing with the clock layout – hours, days or months for each "hour" – or use quarters with one "quarter hour" equaling one week or day or month. This is especially helpful if your client tells you they are looking for guidance on a time-sensitive issue. Use silent intention to establish the timing parameters before the stones are cast.

You can use any of the previous ideas alone, or combine ones that make sense. As you are learning about reading crystals and getting acquainted with your divination stones, it will be helpful to remain consistent in how you read the way the stones fall. The easiest way to do this is to choose one reading layout with one set of "rules" and stick with it for a while. This will provide a framework for learning and give you a higher chance of feeling successful during that learning period.

When doing a private 45 – 60 minute reading, my favorite Crystal or Eclectic Reading method is with the Triple Subject layout. With this layout each colored circle represents a life concern that the client is looking for clarity on. Establish which circle represents which concern by asking your client to name them out loud before casting the crystals. The crystal groupings are read by how they are arranged in each area of concern and the overlapping areas are read as how the concerns interact with or affect each other. The center is of vital importance because it represents the central concern right now. If a crystal lands in the perimeter white area, it could mean that it represents something that doesn't fit within the three subjects, or that it is of lesser importance within the subject it is closest to, or other intuition may come to you about it. When a crystal falls outside the border of the cloth, I usually consider it to be outside the scope of the reading at this time, but some people read those as the most important because they had enough of a charge to be thrown so far. As you practice readings, you will begin to see patterns that will show you how to read your crystals, so don't be intimidated – just start!

A very simple way to do a reading with the Triple Subject layout is to do a past/present/future draw for each subject. After naming the three areas of concern have the client choose (at random from a bag, or by looking at them) three crystals for each subject, laying them out in order in their corresponding circle. Use intuition to give meaning and depth to the reading.

Tarot-Style Layouts

Another way to read Runes and Crystals is with a Tarot-style layout. You can "shuffle" the stones in a bag by gently swishing them around with your fingers and choosing them one at a time. Set them in the order and positions as outlined in the layout you choose.

CONNECTING WITH CRYSTALS

Tarot spreads are great for general readings and easy to find on the web. Two popular 3-card spreads: the Mind-Body-Spirit spread, and the Past-Present-Future spread can be adapted to any stone divination set, but I especially like them with Runes. The combined layout idea below came from www.tarotforum.net. Even though it is a simple concept, the combination of two spreads adds multiple layers of complexity. I love that it uses the magical number 9 from Norse Rune mythology, too.

P....P....F

M...1....4....7

B....2....5....8

S....3....6....9

Lay the stones down in the number order as shown with Mind-Body-Spirit being read across, and Past-Present-Future being read down. Position 1 would be read as past ways of thinking, or mental issues that the client was working on previously. Position 2 would be read as past health situation, and since mind and spirit are already represented, that would mean physical health. Position 3 would be read as past spiritual path, and so on.

You can gain even more insight when you read the diagonals. For instance, 1/5/9 could be read that the past ways of thinking as indicated by the Rune or Crystal in that position have resulted in the client's present physical condition and may influence their spiritual path in the future as suggested by the Rune or Crystal in that position.

Give this combination-spread a try with the reading on the next page by interpreting the Runes I chose in the picture. Use the chart above and this list of meanings from my Fairy Runes set, with the number positions as shown in the picture: 1-Freedom, 2-Prosperity, 3-Trickster, 4-Spirit/Intuition, 5-Grief, 6-Journey/Travel, 7-Reflect, 8-New Direction, 9-Bloom/Grow. Refer to chapter 6 for a full list of my Fairy Runes and their meanings.

Do you have any advice for me? Can you think of a couple different reasons that "Trickster" might show up in my past? Can you tell what stage of life I'm in? To share your insight with me join the *Connecting with Crystals* Facebook group where we can connect with each other!

As you know, there are as many ways to give insightful readings as there are people to read for. My best hope is that you will use these ideas as a creative launching pad to develop your own unique style for accessing the infinite wisdom available to us all.

4

CRYSTALS

Crystals have been recognized throughout time as powerful allies in health and prosperity. Our most ancient written languages contain detailed accounts of the use of crystals for healing, as charms and as protective talismans and they are still in use throughout the world today.

Since the approach of the new millennium there has been a growing interest in using crystals to enhance intuition, promote emotional health and aid physical healing. Stones of all sorts absorb, store and emit energy, but none so effectively as crystals. The fact that crystals have such active energy can make their use in divination an interesting challenge. In working with my own crystals, I have found that some of their meanings have gently shifted over time. Sometimes a crystal that has always meant one thing jumps out as meaning something totally different for just one reading. One of my crystals stopped working altogether and I finally realized that I needed to go through the process of "deep listening" again to learn the new meaning for that crystal. Ironically, it's meaning came forward as "confusion!"

Exploring the realm of Crystals through divination is great fun whether for your own enjoyment or as a profession. In order to master the art of Crystal Divination, though, you will have to be able to consistently access your connection to the Divine through your crystals. The key is in fostering a mutually respectful relationship with them, honoring the spirit in each one...yes, like they are alive!

How I Got Introduced to Crystal Readings

At a small psychic fair in Northwest Washington, I slowly wandered around, checking out the various intuitive offerings. As I was getting a feel for the different readers to see if there was one who seemed like a good fit, I saw something that really got me excited – a crystal layout!

I had never had a Crystal Reading before, so I started a conversation with the reader; Michael Kaminski of Seattle, WA, to see if we would work well together. He seemed very nice and welcoming, so I introduced myself and sat down.

The reading he gave me was powerful – it is so refreshing to be "seen," but what inspired me most was how strongly I connected with the stones. I could feel their energy and it swept me into the psychic realm very quickly. Being trained as a Reiki healer, it made sense to me that the energy of my thoughts and feelings could travel down my arms and through my hands into the crystals and be read when I cast them.

I was also impressed by the fact that Michael didn't simply recite the meanings of the stones and their placements, but used the stones as a portal to the universal information in the psychic realm. Clearly he was a master.

This is the photo I took of our reading.
Visit www.spiritquestacademy.org for more info.

After that reading I couldn't stop thinking about the feeling of connection I shared with those crystals. A couple of weeks went by before I finally decided to do some research online to learn more about crystal readings and a whole world of possibility opened up in me!

As my crystal journey began to take form, I realized that if I was going to master this art I would need a lot of practice. So after creating my first crystal divination set and testing it out on a few close friends, I brought it to some parties and gave lots of free readings in order to speed up my learning process. It helped, certainly, but there is no substitute for time. It takes time to process what you are learning and integrate it into your being in order to have full access to that knowledge. So, practice…yes! But also study, research, touch, play and dream your crystals into your being!

Choosing Crystal Divination Stones

Variety is the spice of life, but when you are selecting crystals for a divination set, the ideal size is 1" to 1½" in diameter, often referred to as "jewelry size" by crystal enthusiasts. This size makes it possible for most people to hold and cast around 12 stones at a time, which is a good number. Twelve stones will cover the ten subjects listed below plus two more that present themselves as important players in your unique set.

An engaging collection of different colors, some clear and some opaque is interesting to work with and useful when you are learning the crystal's meanings.

When considering meanings for your readings, a good place to start is to write down the primary subject areas that you want your readings to be able to address. My first divination set was mostly made up of crystals I already had. I just let their meanings come through without any pre-conceived idea of what I wished for. When I had their meanings and took a look at my set with the desire for a well-rounded reading, I realized that I needed to add a few new colors and subjects. I made a list of the subjects and colors I hoped to find and went to my local crystal shop. I let my desires be loose enough to allow for inspiration and it worked out really well. If you will be searching out all new crystals at a shop, you can create an intention something like this: "I wish to find crystals that match the subject areas I have written down, that work together in harmony and contain a pleasing balance of colors. Thank you." This will help you be open to receiving the best crystals for your unique oracle, because as much as you might want to be in control, sometimes it's best to let the crystals choose you!

Subject Areas to Consider

- LOVE – I often read this as "primary relationship" or the relationship that the client's question is about.

- MONEY – Sometimes this is financial and sometimes more like prosperity or abundance.

- HEALTH – Physical, mental &/or emotional health.

- CHANGE

- CONFUSION

- GREIF – This is sometimes deception, including self-deception, which is common & certainly causes grief!

- HIDDEN POTENTIAL – Or just "potential."

- AMBITION/PASSION

- INTUITION/SPIRITUALITY

- CLARITY/FOCUS

Matching Subject Areas to Crystals

Many people use a crystal encyclopedia or look online (I recommend cross-referencing several sources) to find crystals that match the subject areas they want to use, but I have some highly opinionated opinions about that, which you can read in the next section. What I found most exciting and effective for determining meanings was to use "deep listening" as outlined in Chapter 2.

Here are the meanings that came forward from a set of crystals that I chose at random from one of my *Connecting with Crystals* Kits:

- CLEAR QUARTZ – COSMIC CLARITY, clear knowing, clear communication, pure intuition

- CITRINE – AFFIRMATION, yes, positive illumination

- AMETHYST – FLY, freedom, explore

- ROSE QUARTZ – LOVE, attraction, affiliation

- LAPIS – FORTUNE, prosperity, wealth, bliss

- CARNELIAN – STABILITY, graceful strength, confidence

- AQUAMARINE – SAFETY, security, belonging

- MOONSTONE – SPIRITUAL GUIDANCE

- BLUE LACE AGATE – FRIENDSHIP, connection, business partnership

- BLOODSTONE – HEALTH, body, mind, spirit

- OBSIDIAN – DOUBT, caution

- AMAZONITE – PEAK EXPERIENCE, journey

As I mentioned before, I am clairvoyant, so when I do "deep listening" I see images and the meanings come with them. Often the meanings come in the form of a title with a subset of meanings, but some of the titles on the previous page are simply the dominant attribute with supportive concepts that illustrate the flavor of the actual meaning, or potential meanings during a reading.

Connecting with Crystals Kit, available at: www.JennyClairvoyant.com

The process I used for finding my crystals' meanings was to make a list of their names. I also had a loose list of attributes I wanted to include. I began by tuning in to one of the crystals, but our energies weren't connecting easily, so I decided to clear them all first and invite them to partner with me as a tool to bring understanding through the messages of the Divine. I cleared them with the spoken intention that their surface energies be released into the cosmos to be transformed for the highest and best good, and that they be free to vibrate with their full, natural energies. That did the trick!

About half-way through my crystal-whispering, I thought I would see how I was doing on filling my subject areas. It was going pretty well, but I began to feel like I should be a little more assertive with my own needs for a balanced divination set. I began to feel out the remaining crystals for which ones matched the remaining attributes that I wanted to include and we eventually sorted each other out. During that process I noticed that there were a couple of stones whose meanings weren't coming through easily, so I set them down and came back to them later – it didn't bother me, though, and I did end up understanding their meanings. I kind of think they were waiting to see what meanings were needed closer to the end. Somehow their crystalline structure was more fluid than the others, and therefor they were willing to be somewhat flexible in the meanings they represented. Keep in mind that you are creating a working relationship with energetically active communicators. Being patient and curious encourages them to align with your energy and requests, alternatively, being completely head-over-heels in love with them generates a lasting marriage!

Another thing to consider is what kind of layout or reading style you want to use – it could necessitate the use of certain kinds of crystals. Some readers, like Michael Kaminski, use a large faceted quartz crystal as a centerpiece. Some use a clear crystal "pointer" that either points out where to begin the reading or what the most important part of the reading is. Sometimes crystals are used as markers to delineate sections of the layout, or for determining timing of events that the stones foretell. The layouts I have offered in this book are the ones that I have enjoyed using and seem flexible enough to accommodate multiple techniques of divining with stones.

When creating your crystal oracle, keep in mind that it should not be used for anything else, so if you choose crystals that you already have, make sure you won't be tempted to "borrow" them from your collection. A divination collection becomes a family, and the stones – especially crystals – become very attached to each other.

I already knew this intuitively when I formed my first set, so I always kept them together, but when I was ready to do the photography for this book's cover I really wanted to use the crystals from my Eclectic Collection. As I was separating the actual crystals from the other pieces in my collection I could feel them resisting the separation – they were panicking! I did my best to calm them by explaining what I was doing, but the ones left behind were pretty unhappy. When I brought the crystals back to the rest of the collection, it was like a huge sigh of relief. The crystals from the photo-shoot communicated with the other pieces about their journey and I made a promise to them all that I wouldn't separate them again.

My Opinions on Crystal Meanings and Attributes

For many years I had a book on the magical properties of crystals, gems and metals, but never really felt a kinship with it and chalked it up to my own shortcomings. In time, I came to understand that the reason I didn't feel a connection with that book is that the assertions of meanings and attributes outlined for the stones didn't match the feelings that my stones seemed to have. When I became interested in creating my own Crystal Divination set, I studied several other crystal books and found that some of the attributes associated with some of the crystals vary from book to book depending on what the author understood them to mean.

After thinking it over I came to the conclusion that no author can be the one true authority on meanings for stones that are technically the same stone, but have very different backgrounds in geography and circumstance. It seems that there are certain qualities that some stones are most likely to hold because of their specific crystalline structure, but there are differences in the energies that all stones gather that depend on each one's unique history. These variables would include: where in the world the individual stone came from; what other stones, minerals or metals were near it in the earth as it formed; and the energy of any civilization that was nearby. It is also important to realize that how your stone was gathered from the earth – mined or found, and in what circumstance, may have an effect on its clarity in readings. Being harvested through war-torn mining operations, desert caves or a pristine forest could certainly have an effect on your stone's attributes, although in most cases these energies are absorbed on the surface and can be released as outlined in chapter 2 on Clearing and Charging.

My best advice? If you have a crystal book that you connect with, by all means, use it! If you don't have one, browse your local crystal shop, new age book store, or search the internet to get acquainted with your stones' *potential* attributes. Then connect with each of your crystals in turn, asking them to tell you what attributes they possess. This can come in the form of images that "remind" you of something, or you may experience a feeling or hear a word that seems connected to that stone. If you are already accomplished at deep listening (or even if you aren't) try checking in with your stones first and *then* check other sources to see if the meanings match – this can be a fun game!

5

ECLECTIC COLLECTIONS

What is an Eclectic Divination Collection? Good question. The answer is, "Whatever you put in it!"

I haven't seen any other psychics use an Eclectic Collection of objects for divination, but I say, "Why not?!"

Divination can be accomplished with nearly any tools. Bones have been used in Africa for thousands of years, the I Ching originated from reading the patterns of tortoise shells in ancient China, and Runes were cast by the Vikings. What all divination tools have in common, is the intention of the reader to open a pathway of communication with the Divine flow of universal information, through the tools themselves. As an intuitive reader of Divine communication, the most powerful tools you will ever use are the ones you connect with the most profoundly. So, pay attention to the tools that sweep you away into the blissful abyss of the Divine – they are your doorway to the Universe. By the way, those ancient people made it up as they went along, so we can, too!

When I began my crystal reading journey, I found inspiration in a variety of objects that had been with me for many years. I discovered all kinds of crystals, stones and cherished trinkets tucked away in coat pockets, on shelves, in my car…it was an exciting treasure hunt! I hadn't really realized how much I loved to collect stones until I went searching for them all. That in itself was a powerful message that I was on the right track with making my own Crystal Divination set. Once I had gathered every piece I could find, (including a few that felt like they belonged, but definitely weren't stones) I spent some time with them and thought about whether or not I felt free to dedicate them to my oracle. I considered their sizes, shapes and my connection to them. I wanted my "stones" to be easy to hold and cast, but I also liked the wide variety of shapes, colors, textures and weights of the objects I had collected. I finally narrowed my collection down to about 15 pieces. When I tuned in to my objects to divine each one's meaning, some subject areas (and colors) felt like they were missing, so I went to my local crystal shop and chose several more stones. In the end, twenty seemed like just the right number for me.

At this time, I am unable to share the exact details of which stones match which meanings, but my collection was happy to pose for a "family portrait."

The Eclectic objects in my oracle that are not stones are an interesting variety of natural materials, though some are human-processed. Kwan Yin is brass, the moon-shaped piece is shell and I also use a large pearl. The blue ring has qualities of Aquamarine, but might actually be etched glass. Although it came from a gem shop in Sedona, AZ and the sign said "stone," I'm not actually sure what it is. As I already mentioned, it doesn't seem to matter what objects you use as long as you connect deeply with them and follow the procedures for clearing past energies and charging them with their compatible attributes as outlined in chapter 2.

Maybe it's the fact that most of them were personal treasures before we began working together this way, or maybe it's because they are the first divination crystals I formed as a set, but I am absolutely **in love** with my Eclectic Collection! I think this might be something that "just happens" when you share so much of yourself with your oracle. It took a long time and a lot of readings for our relationship to reach this depth… like a musician's beloved, finely tuned instrument. And even though not all of my Eclectic Collection is stone, I have found that the eclectic objects read just as well as the crystals in my collection, and I wouldn't trade them!

6

RUNES

The word "rune" means mystery, secret or whisper.

Traditional Runes are an ancient set of Norse symbols referred to as "Elder Futhark," but I like the idea of creating uniquely inspired Runes with symbols that have a more personal meaning. Norse Runes were used for divination and magic in addition to writing. As an oracle, Runes were traditionally made from a set of similarly sized and shaped stones or pieces of wood and cast on a white cloth to bring clarity to a question and suggest a possible outcome.

When I was in my late teens I had a friend with a traditional set of Runes and wanted a set very badly, but she told me that the lore of Runes was that it was bad luck to buy them for yourself. "The way the ancients got them was by gift, by theft, or by making their own," she said. Not wanting to do it "wrong" and not knowing anything about creating an oracle of any kind, especially one so steeped in ancient magic, I allowed my imagination to dwell on accidentally dishonoring the ancients and thereby tainting any set that I would make, so I decided to wait until I got them as a gift. Yep, you guessed it… I never got a set! But I eventually got something much more powerful – an understanding of how to access and use pure intention for any application – which freed me from my fears of "doing it wrong."

If you skipped chapter one you might want to read it now, so you can learn how to access pure intention, too.

Gather the Best Stones

You can collect small, flat stones from the river, beach, quarry, or craft store. Try to find ones that are similar in size and shape (1" to 1 ½" diameter is ideal), but variance in color is nice. I like the more natural look for my stones, but if you are really crafty you could probably figure out how to use those medium sized glass marbles with flat bottoms, or a creative re-use idea, like Scrabble tiles. But, no matter what supplies you use for your Runes, make sure you collect them with your full attention on what you are doing. Be open to receiving guidance about the supplies, themselves. Feel them calling to you and honor them by answering.

"I saw the angel in the marble and carved until I set him free."

- Michelangelo

Inscribe your Symbols with Intention

The supplies I use are simple – beach stones and a black fine point permanent ink pen to inscribe the symbols. It's the intention that creates the magic! But, don't let me squash your creativity – you can use any decorating technique you want, as long as it is durable and long-lasting.

While you are drawing your symbols onto each stone, focus on the meaning of the one you are inscribing. Writing, like speaking, can be powerful magic. Allow your intention for the stone to express the symbol's meaning to flow through your heart and into the stone as you inscribe the symbol upon it. When you have finished, hold yourself in a state of gratitude. Thank each stone individually for its service to you and to the highest good, thank the earth for forming the stone, and thank the Spirit(s) for all the guidance you received that brought the stone to you, and brought you to this moment. When your set is complete, hold them all in your hands as you connect with your heart and allow your love to flow into them. Dedicate them to each other as an Oracle. Thank them for working with you and commit yourself to them for the highest purpose and most helpful communication of the Divine.

Choose a Theme

Some examples of themes you might want to use are Elder Futhark Traditional Runes, Fairy Runes, Wiccan Runes, Tarot Runes, or your own Inspired Symbols.

Elder Futhark Traditional Runes

Elder Futhark Runes are made up of a set of 24 symbols with meanings that were important to the Norse people. Opinions vary on the exact meanings of these ancient divination symbols. There are even several versions of Futhark, but the Elder Futhark is thought to be the original set of symbols.

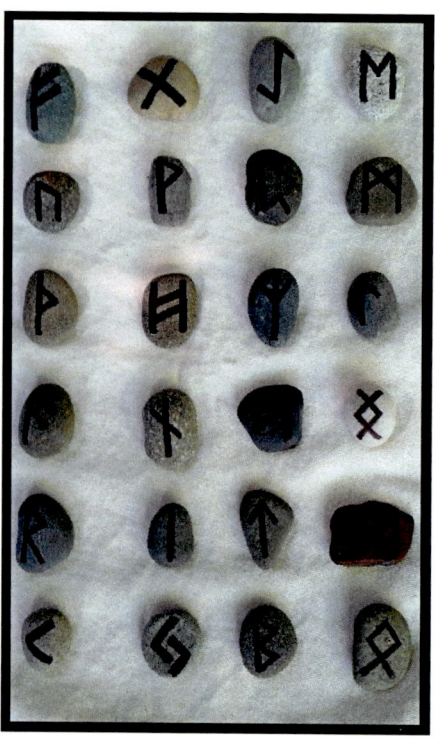

Read across from the top:

Cattle, Gift, Yew Tree, Horse,

Auroch (Wild Ox), Joy, Dice Cup, Humankind,

Thorn or Giant, Hailstone, Elk, Water,

Mouth or Divine Breath, Necessity, Sun, Fertility,

Wheel, Ice, Creator, Day,

Torch, Harvest, Birch Tree, Home

The *Book of Runes* by Ralph Blum is a good companion to any traditional set of Runes, be they store bought or hand made. It is easy to find online with over 2 million copies in print, but as Dan McCoy of norse-mythology.org put it, "What you learn from the runes directly, through experience and intuitive insight, is always more important than anything you read in a **book**." I must say that I very much agree!

Fairy Runes

Create an expression of your connection with the Fairy Realm. Consider the attributes and personalities of the Fairies you know and make a list of the concepts that are important to *them*. If you don't feel that you communicate with Fairies, just allow all that you love about what they represent to enter your thoughts. When I made my set of 13 Fairy Runes, I thought about how to incorporate concepts that were important to me in addition to ones that I thought needed expression in an intuitive reading, with concepts that I thought had value to Fairies. This is what I came up with:

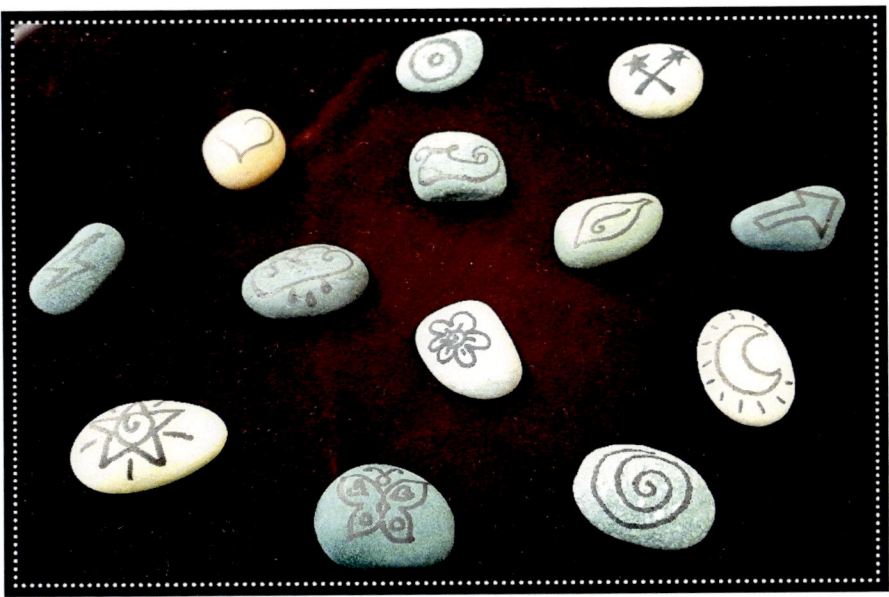

Create a symbol and description for each of your concepts and then modify them until you are comfortable with your set. You may use any quantity of symbols you like, but consider that sometimes "less is more." I have found that it can be easier to connect to intuition if there is *less* to distract me in the physical realm leaving *more* intuitive space for Spiritual Guidance. So, I ended up with 13 Runes; enough for the 9-tile layouts in this book, an easy number of symbols to remember, and about the maximum you would want to hold in your hands when casting them.

- Butter-Fairy-Fly: Freedom
- Flower: Bloom/Grow
- Leaf: True Nature
- Crossed Wands: Trickster
- Lightning Bolt: Flash Flood/Storm
- Heart: Love/Relationship
- Rain Cloud: Grief
- Double Circles: Prosperity
- Arrow: New Direction
- Moon: Reflect
- Sun Star: Strength/Power
- Elf Boot: Travel/Journey
- Spiral: Spirit/Intuition

When you are ready to implant your symbols into your Runes, be thoughtful about the stone you choose for each symbol. Use your intuition to feel which stone by asking the stones, "which one is for this symbol?" as you point to the first symbol and reach out to the stones with a clear intention that the stone that is the best fit for that symbol will clearly get your attention, rather than thinking with your logical brain. When you have chosen your first stone, focus on the meaning of the symbol you are drawing and use intention as described in the previous section called, "Inscribe your Symbols with Intention." When you have finished, remember to thank the Fairies for all the guidance they provided in the creation of your Fairy Runes and in your life.

Wiccan Runes

Wiccan Runes are a collection of magickal symbols from the Wiccan tradition. Many Wiccans use traditional Runes for divination, but there are so many possibilities. Consider the meanings of the many occult symbols and how they could be used as a tool for divination. Write down your divination interpretations and if needed, create your own additional symbols or add crystals to complete your set. You can also use the ideas for creating Fairy Runes as a template. Remember, all of the symbols created in ancient times were created by someone. You embody that same creative spirit and I encourage you to use it!

Tarot Runes

This is an interesting concept considering that some authorities believe that Tarot Cards originated from the Elder Futhark…full circle! You can use the Major Arcana of Tarot by modifying the symbolism for each card. You might also choose to simply use the Major Arcana number for each Rune, or choose both – use a modified symbol for one side of the Rune and the corresponding number on the other side.

Finding attributes that match the Minor Arcana in crystals is one idea of how you could complete your Tarot Rune "deck" for in-depth readings and you could easily separate them from the Runes for less complex readings. There are many creative ideas to explore here, so trust your intuition!

Inspired Runes

Inspired Runes are a collection of symbols inspired by you. My set of Inspired Runes represent concepts I feel are important for a good reading and ones that have value to me. Consider the kinds of questions you would want clarity on in a reading and then imagine the best descriptions for reaching resolution and gaining insight. Draw your inspired symbols out on paper with the descriptions next to them and modify them until you are comfortable with your set. It may take a few hours, or a few days' work before you are ready to literally set them in stone, so be open to however your process unfolds.

CONNECTING WITH CRYSTALS

My Inspired Runes set has 16 stones:

- Seed About to Come Up: Hidden Potential
- Circle with Dot: Protection
- Sun: Illumination
- Eye with Teardrop: Grief
- Heart & Arrows: Connection
- Moon: Reflection
- Hand: Healing
- Yin/Yang: Balance
- Rippling Lines: Flow
- Circle with Slash: Let Go
- Spiral: Intuition
- Horizon Line: Earth
- Dollar Sign: Wealth
- Heart: Love
- Kitty Cat: Instinct
- Fountain: Spirituality

I have loved this set of Inspired Runes, but I do have one regret. Instead of making a cheat-sheet with the symbols and meanings, I wrote the meanings on the backs. Most of the stones were too small to fit the words and it just ended up looking messy. Consequently, I only use them for myself. It's true that I could make another set with the same symbols, but then what would I do with my first ever divination set of super special, meaning-infused Inspired Runes?

Discarding Divination Stones

I actually prefer to use the term "releasing" when the situation arises. It adds an element of respect that our Divine tools deserve.

When you are creating a tool for Divination, that is, a tool for communicating with the Divine Consciousness, you are obliged to maintain a state of reverence. Reverence can range from solemnity to flamboyantly wild exultations; it is the intention and attention that creates reverence. Likewise, when you are releasing a Divining tool you are equally obliged to do this with at least the same level of reverence as when creating it, even if your stone is only partly created. So, chucking your "mistake" stones in the garbage is out of the question!

The way to release a Divine messenger is to choose an appropriate place to retire the stone, then tune in to your heart connection and say something like this:

"Thank you beach stone for your willingness to participate with me in Divine communication. I now return you to the shore, releasing you from any further obligation and sending you back out into the world for your next adventure. May your continued connection with the Divine be for the highest and best good in the Universe."

Sometimes, just the act of returning an object that has been used as a ritual item to its natural environment (or even one that is unintentionally infused with emotional attachments) can break those bonds, especially when done with the intention of release.

A Personal Story of Release

When we were dating, my first husband gave me a rock with a beautiful double heart etched into the top of it by the water of the flowing stream that he found it in. I kept it all the years we were together and then ran across it about five years after our divorce.

Finding that rock at that time was not accidental. We had been entrenched in child custody difficulties for many years and about that time I had shifted my focus from trying to make him "see reason," to letting go of my need for him to act in a way that I thought was reasonable. I thought about what to do with that rock. Should I save it for our daughter as proof that there had once been love between us? Should I chuck it into the woods and forget about it? Then it dawned on me that I had to give it back.

The next kid-swap was at the ferry terminal, so I brought it with me and offered it up in the most sincere and disarming way possible, but he refused to take it! I knew I couldn't keep it, so the only obvious thing to do was to return it to water. Puget sound is a lot different than a fresh-flowing stream, but, well, there it was…and the time was "right now." I walked out to the end of the pier where no one else was and although I didn't say any words, not even silently to myself, my intention for release was extremely clear as I threw the "love rock" as far into the water as I could.

I did have one silent hope as I walked away: that the swishing water and the flow of the tides would wash away all the hurt, and in time, the love would be clear and clean again. Our daughter is an adult now, and just months ago her father and I attended her college graduation, after not seeing each other for about 10 years. The year previous, he had reached out to me with an apology which I very much appreciated, and responded to with my own apology. My silent hope was satisfied…at least to a degree.

Re-Assigning Divination Stones

If you like your divination stones, but don't want to use them anymore for doing readings, you could choose to give them another job. You could "plant" them in your garden to stimulate growth, place them near the entrance to your home for protection, or tuck them under your bed with an intentional request for something you are wanting to manifest in your life. This re-direction of energy is most effective when you consult your stones to make sure that they are on board with their new job. The way you can tell how they feel is by opening a connection with them – with intention of course! Make your request for the re-direction you are proposing and then see if you can feel a gentle pull "toward," or a feeling of resistance. I often feel resistance as a prickly feeling on my skin, or the hairs on the back of my neck standing up. A happy pull feels like a gentle whoosh toward the new idea. If you feel stuck, just try stuff out and see where your intuition leads you. If your heart is open and clear, you won't "do it wrong." Trust the stones to tell you what you need to know, and trust yourself to listen.

I relate to all stones as if they are living beings. They feel alive to me! Their energy has a vibration that I easily connect with and they share their "voice" with me through feelings and words that come into my mind in almost the same way that I receive information from Spirit Beings. To deepen your connection, try carrying your Runes in your pocket, sleep with them under your pillow, or sing to them. Soon they will also sing to you.

7

GIVING READINGS

Whether you decide to give readings only to friends and family, or you take up lithomancy as a profession, there are some significant aspects to giving readings that you should be aware of. This chapter covers some stories and ideas about how to get started with giving readings and your ethical responsibilities as a person who is giving Divine counsel. There is an art to giving a good reading – from getting out of your head to creative consistency – but the most important aspect to being a good reader is to uphold a strong dedication to ethics.

After forming my first divination set, I played around with it a bit by myself. I practiced by casting them in my little ribbon circle, learning the stones' meanings and trying to figure out what the meanings might be when they were in clusters. At first it can feel kind of robotic and repetitious as you work on the memorization of your Rune symbols, Crystal names, and their meanings. Trying to memorize your oracle's meanings keeps you in your head, making it harder to connect with intuition. But don't let yourself get discouraged, just accept that this is the beginning of the giving-readings-learning-curve and keep going!

After establishing some basic "rules" for how I was going to read the stones and cast them, I practiced on a couple of really good friends that I thought would be supportive no matter how it went. Here is where I must confess. I had to use a cheat-sheet for my first 15-20 readings because I didn't do my memorization homework first. If you are like me and have a natural tendency to jump first and look second, just know that it is best to do as much solitary practice as you can stand before you start offering readings to others. Constantly referring to a cheat-sheet does not inspire confidence in your abilities!

When I decided to try giving readings to more people, I asked my friend, who had invited me to her girl-party, if I could bring my divination set and offer free readings. She agreed, even though she seemed somewhat dubious, so I was careful to wait until the party was on the down-swing before setting up my stones and offering readings. I knew that I was not the main event at the party and felt that it was important to be respectful.

Ethic #1 – Respect

Respect is a multi-faceted gem:

- Self-Respect: Respect your own emotional state, if you're having a really rough day, don't go spreading that around in readings. If you are having physical problems, just be aware that strong subliminal distractions can affect readings.

- Limitations: Respect your own limitations and be honest.

You are not omnipotent. Present yourself in your true light – which is amazing just how it is! (No apology needed!)

- Environment: Respect the environment you are in and the people you are with by not forcing an opportunity for readings, or even talking about it when it is not being encouraged. Engage, to be sure, but respect other's rights to maintain their fear-responses while gently explaining that your readings are for the highest good – threats and scare-tactics are not your style! (Because you uphold a high level of ethics!)

- Client: Respect the "space" your client is in. They will hear whatever they are ready to hear – you can't make them understand. Just give them the best reading you can, the rest is up to them.

As a general rule I don't do readings under the influence of alcohol because it muddies the lines between true intuition and my own opinions and conclusions, but for my first few readings it took a couple of glasses of wine for me to pluck up the courage to ask my friends if they wanted a reading: "Hey, I just happened to bring my divination set with me, do you want a reading?" So, do whatever it takes to get yourself out of the psychic closet, but know that a clear head provides the highest level of honesty and is the most reliable kind of head to have when you are acting as a Divine Messenger.

Ethic #2 – Clarity

Be clear and clean while you are acting as a Divine Messenger:

- Getting High: Don't do alcohol or drugs when you are giving readings. I, like Shamans of many different cultures, have done hallucinogenic drugs for Spirit Journeying and it can be an amazing experience. But it is not a state in which one gives Divine counsel. Being on any drug, including alcohol, is a solitary journey. Being a Divine Messenger is a cooperative journey. Being clear and clean for readings shows that you honor the difference.

Ethic #3 – Advice

Don't ever* give advice, especially medical advice!

- *Ever: What the heck?! Yes, that's right, never give advice…unless you are a licensed Counselor or other Mental Health Provider, Ordained Clergy, or are legally licensed to give the kind of advice you are giving.

- Pass the buck: When I give readings, I say things like: "…the information that is coming to me from Spirit Realm is…" or "…what the stones are saying is…" or "…the images I am being shown are _____, but you should get a second opinion from someone with letters after their name!" (I often get a laugh with that one!)

- Opportunist BS: Never take advantage of a vulnerable person, or a person who is in a vulnerable emotional state. For instance: telling them they should consult you again tomorrow because some bad thing is going to happen, or taking pre-payment and then not giving what you promised, or lying about information you are receiving to get them to consult you again. It pains me to have to include this, but it is a real thing that some inauthentic people do. It undermines those of us who are authentic and perpetuates a feeling of mistrust for all kinds of intuitives.

Ethic #4 – Confidentiality

Confidentiality means that whatever happens or is said during a session is absolutely confidential.

- What to say: Nothing! You really have no idea who knows whom, so thinking that you are acting confidentially while telling someone about a session you just had, and simply leaving out the client's name, is not going to cut it. How would you feel if you were talking with an acquaintance who told you a story that they heard from your psychic reader and it turned out to be your private story? You could pretend that it wasn't your story, but would you ever go back to that reader? Would you tell your friends good things about that reader? Not likely.

- Permission: If, like me, you feel drawn to sharing stories for the learning opportunities they provide, you could ask your clients for permission to tell their story. A signed permission form is the best kind, but email agreement is also legal. Even when I have permission to tell a story, I always leave out identifying information unless I am given express permission and even encouragement to use a person's name or other potentially identifying information.

Ethics are of utmost importance, but it is also important to remember that life is supposed to be fun! So smile and laugh, and find the positive influences in each reading, even if there are obstacles for your client to overcome. It is your responsibility to spread love, light and hope – I have faith in you!

Glossary

Divination – the art or practice that seeks to foresee or foretell future events or discover hidden knowledge usually by the interpretation of omens or by the aid of supernatural powers.

Eclectic – deriving ideas, style, or taste from a broad and diverse range of sources.

Ethics – moral principles that govern a person's or group's behavior.

Lithomancy – divination by means of stones or stone talismans.

Oracle – Back in ancient times, an oracle was someone who offered advice or a prophecy thought to have come directly from a divine source. In this book the stones themselves are often referred to as an oracle.

Reiki – a discipline of alternative medicine using healing energy with a technique commonly called palm healing or hands-on-healing.

Spirit Being – a supernatural **being** or essence: an incorporeal **being.**

Spirit Realm – the region, sphere, or domain within which spirits exist.

Bibliography & Resources

Paul O'Brien, http://divination.com (History of Divination)

Ingrid Halverson, www.sunnyway.com/runes (Runes, general)

Dan Gronitz, www.therunesite.com (Runes, meanings)

Dan McCoy, http://norse-mythology.org (Runes)

Kate Hill, Aeclectic Tarot, www.tarotforum.net (Tarot layouts)

Michael Kaminski, www.spiritquestacademy.org (Crystal Readings)

Gary Wimmer, www.garywimmer.com (Lithomancy)

Jenny Jo Allen, www.JennyClairovyant.com (Guided Audio Meditations, *Connecting with Crystals* Workshops & Kits)

Avatar the Last Airbender, http://www.imdb.com/title/tt0417299/ (Wise Entertainment)

MEET THE AUTHOR

Portrait Photo Credit: Diane Isaacs
All Other Photos: Jenny Jo Allen & Joseph Bayley

Jenny Jo Allen is a Clairvoyant Psychic Medium, Reiki Master and Medical Intuitive. She offers *Connecting with Crystals* workshops, DIY kits, private sessions, and is available for speaking engagements. In addition to adventure travel, Jenny enjoys crafting while tucked cozily into her Northwest Washington log cabin with her family and kitty-cat.

Stay connected: www.Facebook.com/JennyClairvoyant.
Learn more about Jenny's work: www.JennyClairvoyant.com.

Made in the USA
San Bernardino, CA
11 February 2018